INSPECTOR ROCKFORT

& the missing treasure

Judith Rossell

A Division of Sterling Publishing Co., Inc.
New York

Inspector Rockfort and his young assistant, Nat, were in their office when the phone rang. It was Professor Pyramid, the curator of the town museum.

"Twelve of our most precious treasures have been stolen from the Egyptian collection!" he said. "Please come at once!"

"We'll be right there," the detective promised. He hung up the phone and turned to his assistant. "We've got a case to solve, Nat—let's go see Professor Pyramid."

"I can already see five pyramids right here in this room," Nat replied.

At the museum, Professor Pyramid showed the detectives photos of the stolen objects.

"A witness saw the thief run out of the museum with a big bag and disappear down a street of shops," the curator explained. "The empty bag was found at the end of the street—but there was no sign of the treasure."

Inspector Rockfort and Nat stepped out onto the street.

"Very curious," said the inspector. "Look, Nat, I can see one of the missing pieces—the blue scarab. The thief must have hidden it, and is planning to come back for it later. My guess is we will find all the stolen objects along this street. Let's start by interviewing the shopkeepers."

"I can't see the hidden scarab," said Nat, "but I can see ten hidden stars."

Mrs. Floss, Candy Store

"Mrs. Floss," said Inspector Rockfort, "we are investigating a robbery at the museum."

"What a coincidence," said Mrs. Floss. "I think I've been robbed, too. I'm missing six red-and-yellow lollipops."

"Don't worry," said the inspector. "I can see them all here in this room."

"And I can see ten carrots," Nat added.

Ms. Rotunda, Junk Shop

"What excellent timing, Inspector," said Ms. Rotunda. "I hope you can help me. All my clocks are either broken or wrong—except two. Which two are showing the right time?"

"Hmm," said Inspector Rockfort, "two clocks showing the same time…"

"Aha!" said Nat. "There are ten elephants in this shop!"

Mr. Rambutan, Fruit Shop

"Good morning, Mr. Rambutan," said Inspector
Rockfort. "We're here to investigate—"

"Ah, Detective, thank goodness you're here. My
last delivery of mangoes contained ten tropical fruit
snails, and now they are loose in the shop! Please
help me find them before they eat all my stock."

"Gladly," said the inspector.

"That's funny," said Nat. "I can't see any snails, but
I can see ten fish."

Ms. Swoon, Art Gallery

"Ah, Inspector Rockfort. How convenient. I recently purchased these seven paintings, as I was told they were the work of Otto Spotto (1853-1890), who always painted exactly from life. But now I suspect they may be fakes!"

Inspector Rockfort studied the paintings carefully. "Yes," he said. "Unfortunately, they are all fakes. They were not painted by Otto Spotto—and there is a mistake in each one."

"I don't know much about art," admitted Nat, "but I can see ten pencils in this shop."

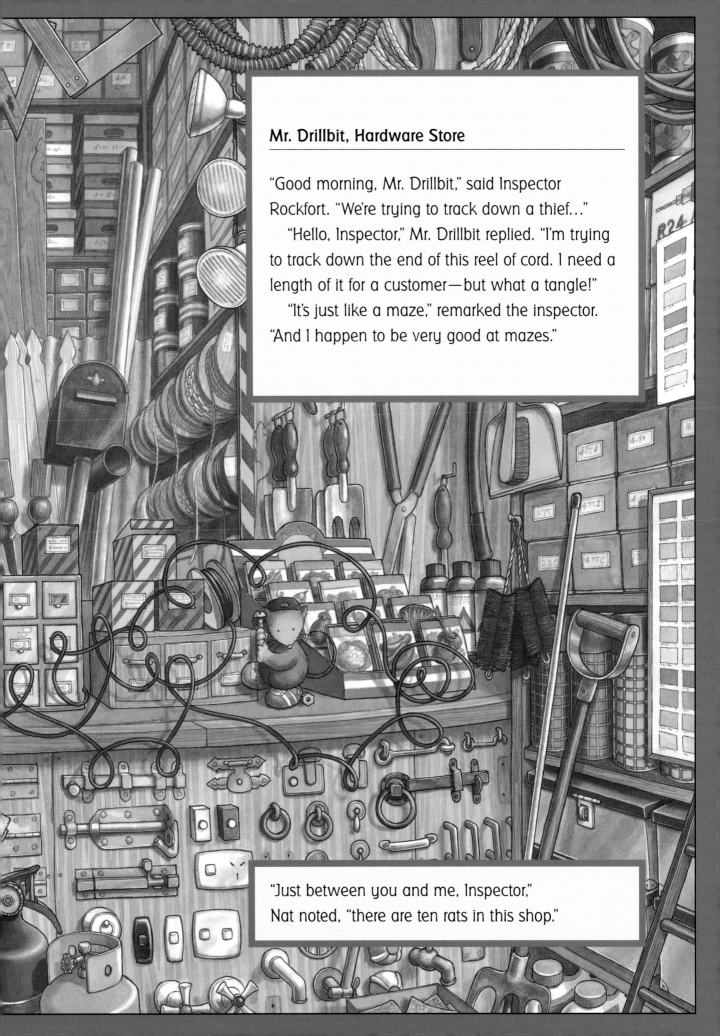

Mr. Drillbit, Hardware Store

"Good morning, Mr. Drillbit," said Inspector Rockfort. "We're trying to track down a thief…"

"Hello, Inspector," Mr. Drillbit replied. "I'm trying to track down the end of this reel of cord. I need a length of it for a customer—but what a tangle!"

"It's just like a maze," remarked the inspector. "And I happen to be very good at mazes."

"Just between you and me, Inspector," Nat noted, "there are ten rats in this shop."

Mr. Friz, Ice-Cream Parlor

"Ah, welcome," said Mr. Friz. "You know, Inspector, I love ice cream. Every day, I make myself a delicious sundae, with one scoop of ice cream, some topping, and a little biscuit. Now, I have five flavors of ice cream, four toppings and three kinds of biscuit. How many different sundaes can I make?"

"Let me see…" said Inspector Rockfort.

"Maybe we need to taste all the sundaes," suggested Nat.
"But Mr. Friz, why are there ten seals in your shop?"

Mrs. Figg, Toy Store

"Good morning, Mrs. Figg," said Inspector Rockfort. "We—"

"Oh, Inspector!" interrupted Mrs. Figg. "Someone raced through the shop and made me drop all these boxes. Now I have to put all the puzzles back together. But which are the two missing pieces of this jigsaw?"

"I'm sure I can help you," said Rockfort. "I like puzzles."

"There are a lot of sheep in this shop," said Nat. "I can see ten."

Mr. Angus, China Shop

"You're just in time, Inspector," said Mr. Angus. "Mrs. Hopper wants to buy a present for a friend who doesn't like flowers, fruit, spots, stripes, or anything red or green. Can you help me find something?"

"What a picky friend!" said Inspector Rockfort. "Luckily, I can see three things that would be suitable."

"Inspector," called Nat. "Did you notice the ten turtles in this shop?"

"Well, we've recovered all the stolen treasures, Nat," Rockfort said. "But the thief is still walking free in this very square. All that remains is to put him behind bars."

"How are we going to do that?" asked Nat. "We don't have any proof!"

"Oh, yes we do," said Rockfort. "The thief left pieces of evidence behind in every shop. Did you see them?"

SEARCH · SEEK · SOLVE · SOLUTIONS

- The missing treasures (the thief hid one in each shop)
- The hidden shapes spotted by Nat (there are actually 11, not 10!)

The Street

Mrs. Floss, Candy Store

Ms. Rotunda, Junk Shop

Mr. Rambutan, Fruit Shop

Ms. Swoon, Art Gallery

Mr. Drillbit, Hardware Store